Rainy Day Unicorn Fun

A Phoebe and Her Unicorn Activity Book

Dana Simpson

Andrews McMeel
PUBLISHING®

Rainy Day Unicorn Fun

Andrews McMeel Publishing
a division of Andrews McMeel Universal
1130 Walnut Street, Kansas City, Missouri 64106

www.andrewsmcmeel.com

22 23 24 25 26 SDB 10 9 8 7 6 5

ISBN: 978-1-4494-8725-6

Made by:
King Yip (Dongguan) Printing & Packaging Factory Ltd.
Address and location of manufacturer:
Daning Administrative District, Humen Town
Dongguan Guangdong, China 523930
5th Printing—5/16/22

All puzzles copyright Puzzler Media Ltd and supplied under
license from Puzzler Media Ltd- www.puzzler.com.

ATTENTION: SCHOOLS AND BUSINESSES
Andrews McMeel books are available at quantity
discounts with bulk purchase for educational, business, or
sales promotional use. For information, please e-mail the
Andrews McMeel Publishing Special Sales Department:
specialsales@amuniversal.com.

1

Kriss Kross

Once you have fitted all the words correctly into the grid, the highlighted letters, when rearranged, will spell out something to do with Phoebe.

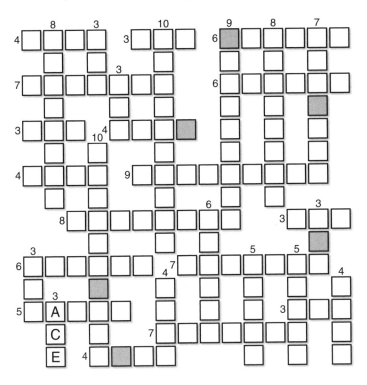

3 letters	4 letters	6 letters	8 letters
~~ACE~~	DESK	DEDUCE	DOVETAIL
ARC	FARO	GOVERN	MULBERRY
CUD	GRIP	NEATER	REFORMAT
HUT	HAKE	RITUAL	
ITS	JIBE		**9 letters**
NUB	PEAK	**7 letters**	DIGNITARY
PHI		ATTACHE	ELEVATION
TOE	**5 letters**	BULBOUS	
USE	ALLOW	CARAVAN	**10 letters**
	BASIC	OFFICER	COQUETTISH
	HOUSE		UNRESOLVED

2
Quest

All the answers to the clues are four-letter words, and you have to enter them into the grid, starting from the outer squares. When you have done that, you will find a party item reading clockwise around the innermost squares starting with number 9.

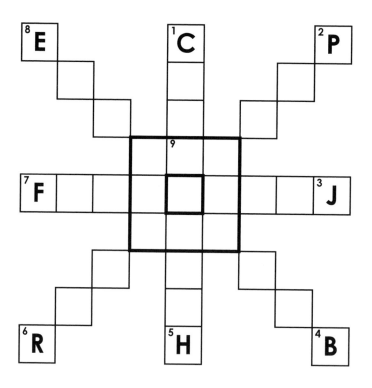

1 Potato _____
2 Large wild American cat
3 Army vehicle
4 Sky color
5 Sixty minutes
6 Wealthy
7 Jumping insect that annoys cats and dogs
8 Way out

3
Tony's Pants

Which path should Tony take to get to his pants?

4
Spot the Difference

Can you spot the eight differences?

5
Number jig

Fit all the listed series of numbers into the grid.

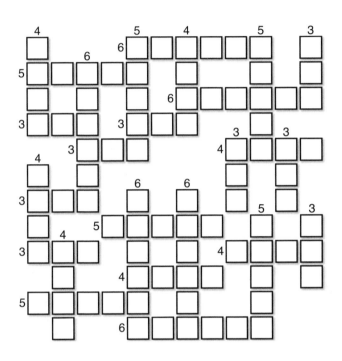

3 digits	4 digits	5 digits	6 digits
116	1743	18183	251182
165	3375	47684	315776
266	3550	76243	572947
301	3896	76758	772053
350	8337	85854	908067
352	9100	93445	987042
417	9821		
536			
928			

6
Suguru & Set Square

Suguru: Each cell in an outlined block must contain a number: A two-cell block contains the numbers 1 and 2; a three-cell block contains the numbers 1, 2, and 3; and so on. The same number must not appear in neighboring cells, not even diagonally.

	3		1		1
					4
3					

***

Set Square: Place each of the numbers 1–9 in the grid to make the sums work. We've started you with two numbers.

	x		÷	2	= 10
x		x		+	
	x		x		= 18
+		+		x	
	x	7	x		= 504

= 21   = 37   = 24

7
Crosswords

Once you have completed the crossword, rearrange the highlighted letters to spell out something to do with Phoebe.

ACROSS
1 Mound, pile (4)
3 Framed lenses to help eyesight (10)
10 Cinema film (5)
11 Fortify, shore up (9)
12 Washington headquarters of the US armed forces (8)
13 Sheep's coat of wool (6)
15 Bandage material (5)
16 Cartoon-film maker (8)
19 ___ Granger, Harry Potter's friend (8)
21 Topic of discussion (5)
23 More than allowed (6)
25 Area for tents (8)
27 Rock group's string musician (9)
28 Holder, possessor (5)
29 Short plank you ride on (10)
30 Fishing-net material (4)

DOWN
1 Main screen of a website (4,4)
2 Exciting experience (9)
4 Coffee maker (10)
5 Piece of metal, used as money (4)
6 Fodder crop (7)
7 Opposite of "little" (5)
8 Country, capital Stockholm (6)
9 Conduct oneself properly (6)
14 Something that prevents you from finishing a job (4-6)
17 Act of doing as you are told (9)
18 Background reading and study (8)
20 Information passed on (7)
21 Walk quietly (6)
22 Lines of bushes around a field (6)
24 Fine delicate pottery (5)
26 Chauffeur-driven car, for short (4)

8
Change a Letter

Solve the clues below, changing one letter of your answer at a time. When you get to clue 12, you'll find that its answer is also one letter different from the first answer—PALE.

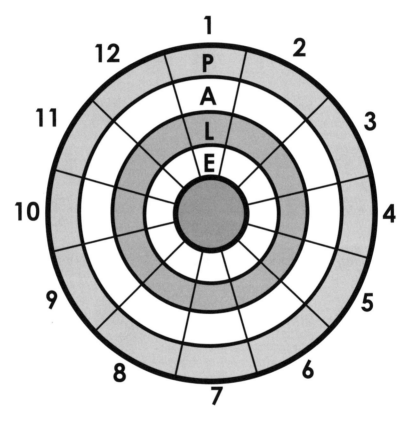

1 Light colored
2 Story
3 Chat
4 Go on foot
5 Brick barrier
6 Bouncy toy
7 Door chime
8 Prison room
9 Be a snitch
10 Cash register
11 Capsule
12 Heap

9
Mythical Creatures

Can you find all the mythical creatures hidden in the grid?

```
A R E M I H C D I A M R E M D
T S T D S T S B E P I Y N U B
A T K R A K E N A T C D A S E
O T U O E A W S O S I C D L M
T X A L G S E O T A I R F E O
N N P W H R R Y U E C L P D N
L I L E P R E C H A U N I S G
E H L S A O W T P M I E N S U
C P A M S E O O L L E T N N K
E S H G E T L A B E B O I I E
N Y C O R R F O H D G C N F P
T R R O E H G S S A O U O F I
A T L I E N N A R R Y E T I X
U L L N A A I D N R E I S R I
R O A T B F Y X E C D L R G E
```

BANSHEE
BASILISK
BUNYIP
CENTAUR
CHIMERA
DRAGON
ELF
FAIRY
GNOME

GOBLIN
GREMLIN
GRIFFIN
IMP
KELPIE
KRAKEN
LEPRECHAUN
MERMAID
OGRE

PHOENIX
PIXIE
SPHINX
SPRITE
TROLL
UNICORN
WEREWOLF
YETI

10

Cross Out

Each of the squares in this grid contains two letters. Can you cross out one letter in each square so that the remaining letters spell out words in all rows and columns? We've crossed out the D in the top left-hand square to start you off.

D̶ T	O R	A O	R I	S N
O W	Z D		U Y	
P R	R I	D O	E U	D R
I C	I E		O S	
H C	H O	E R	S F	U E

Junior Sudoku

Fill in the grids so each row, column, and 2 x 3 block contains the digits 1–6.

			6	2	1
			5	4	
				6	4
6	3			1	
4	6	3	1		
5		1			

			5	2	
		2			3
	4	1		5	6
	5	3		4	2
		5			4
			2	3	

	6			3	
			6		2
5	3			6	
		6			
6			3		1
1	4		2		

12

Picture Pairs

Can you find the two identical pictures?

13
Count Up

How many bats can you find jumbled up in this picture?

Dot to Dot

Join the dots from 1 to 110 to reveal the picture.

Kriss Kross

Once you have fitted all the words correctly into the grid, the highlighted letters will spell out something to do with how Phoebe and Marigold became friends.

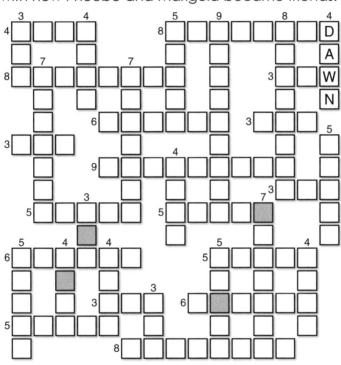

3 letters
CAB
COD
DEW
GUN
INK
TUG
USE
YES

4 letters
COLD
DAWN
DUKE
GATE
ROTE
RUSH
UNDO

5 letters
AIRER
ALDER
DECOR
DOWSE
GASSY
SIDES
STOVE
SWEEP

6 letters
ADJUST
DRUDGE
MOUSSE

7 letters
ABASHED
ANOTHER
PERTURB

8 letters
BACKHAND
INSCRIBE
ORDINARY
SCAFFOLD

9 letters
ADDRESSEE
CHORISTER

16
Pick Me Up

Can you decide in what order you would pick up the popsicle sticks if you could only remove the top one each time?

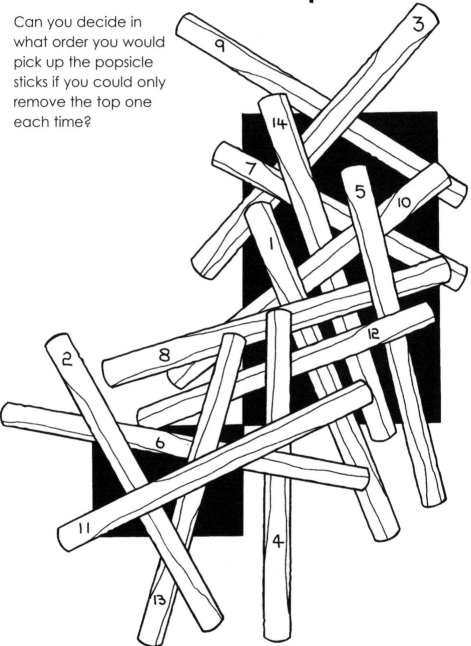

17

Quest

All the answers to the clues are four-letter words, and you have to enter them into the grid, starting from the outer squares. When you have done that, you will find a style of dancing reading clockwise around the innermost squares starting with number 9.

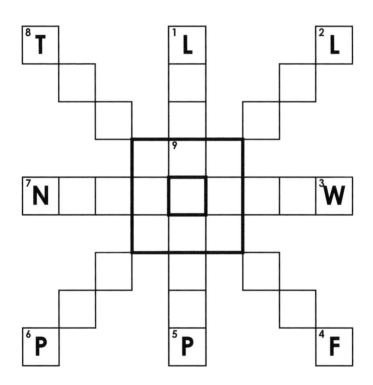

1 Young sheep
2 Bart Simpson's brainy sister
3 Brick barrier
4 Young horse
5 Not rich
6 Sport played on horseback
7 Finding ___, animated fish film
8 Part of a school year

18
Strictly Ballroom

The twenty moves that make up the Random Fandango are pictured below.

The number on each footprint indicates how many moves to make, while the letters provide the direction (D for Down, U for Up, L for Left, and R for Right).

If the "black star" step is the last move to make, which is the first?

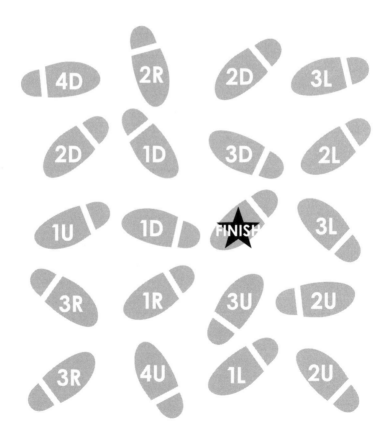

Magic Boxes

In a magic box, the words read the same across and down, as in the sample below.

Make three more magic boxes using the words listed below and make sure that the word LATE appears in each box.

M	A	L	T
A	F	A	R
L	A	T	E
T	R	E	K

AXEL	MEMO	LATE
LATE	PILL	TEAM
IDEA	LEFT	ELMS
ATOM	LATE	SLAM

Suguru & Set Square

Suguru: Each cell in an outlined block must contain a number: A two-cell block contains the numbers 1 and 2; a three-cell block contains the numbers 1, 2, and 3; and so on. The same number must not appear in neighboring cells, not even diagonally.

	4			1	4
	2				2
					5
	3				5

***

Set Square: Place each of the numbers 1–9 in the grid to make the sums work. We've started you with two numbers.

5	x		+		= 19
+	■	x	■	x	
8	-		x		= 42
+	■		-	■	+
	÷		+		= 15
= 19		= 5		= 37	

21
Tongue Twister

Can you work out which of these boys is licking the lollipop?

Jack   Ben   Henry

22
Broom, Broom

Wanda the witch has found her book of spells, but now she's lost her broomstick. Can you find eight of them hidden in the picture?

Change a Letter

Solve the clues below, in order, changing one letter of your answer each time to make a new word to fit the next clue. When you get round to clue 12, you will find that its answer is just one letter different from the first answer—FEEL.

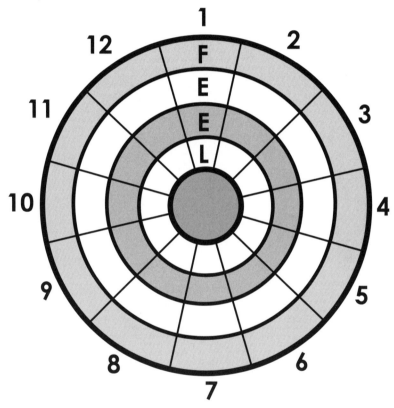

1 ~~Touch~~
2 Paws, hooves
3 Come face to face with
4 Beef, pork, etc.
5 Castle's water barrier
6 Complain
7 Amount of money borrowed
8 Slant, tilt
9 Nasty, unkind
10 Dinner, breakfast, etc.
11 Ring out like bells
12 Fruit skin

24
Spot the Difference

Can you spot the eight differences?

25
Number jig

Fit all the listed series of numbers into the grid.

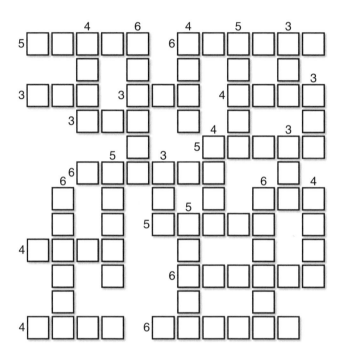

3 digits	4 digits	5 digits	6 digits
107	2437	21486	146372
310	4659	33969	233384
526	6837	59754	233526
655	7003	66337	404620
823	7004	75176	873668
871	9018	90243	942898
915	9561		945343
957			

Cross Out

Each of the squares in this crossword grid contains two letters. Can you cross out one letter in each square so that the remaining letters spell out words in all rows and columns? We've crossed out the M in the top left-hand square to start you off.

M L	E O	L M	O L	Y N
I A	A	A R		I E
P L	I L	A N	E I	T N
L A	G	G C		W T
C E	L P	H O	G T	H O

Crosswords

Once you have completed the crossword, rearrange the highlighted letters to spell out something to do with Marigold.

ACROSS

1 Country with a monarch (7)
5 Birthday-cake light (6)
10 Conditions of a game (5)
11 Appreciation, thanks (9)
12 Stated publicly (9)
13 Be in a huff (4)
15 Trustworthy, truthful (6)
17 Glide on frozen water (3-5)
20 Event occurring not on purpose (8)
21 Sporting ploy (6)
22 Sound of a stone falling into water (4)
24 Middle or later part of the day (9)
28 Conductor's group of musicians (9)
29 Field of sporting contests (5)
30 Touched with the lips (6)
31 Birthday gift (7)

DOWN

1 Kim ___, US reality TV celebrity (10)
2 Material often used for hosiery (5)
3 Talked about (9)
4 Supernatural power (5)
6 Also known as (5)
7 Pair of entertainers (6,3)
8 Balanced and level (4)
9 Field for horses (7)
14 Later family member (10)
16 Strings of beads (9)
18 Domestic series of steps (9)
19 Dig up, discover (7)
23 Bit, fragment (5)
25 Lady and the ___, Disney film (5)
26 Very overweight (5)
27 Hardback or paperback (4)

Hidden Words

The name of a young animal is hidden among the words in each of the sentences below. Can you find all six?

1 Many local folk raise money for charity.
2 Mind you don't skid on the ice.
3 Don't let the door slam behind you.
4 Scuba diving is great fun.
5 A chic kaftan is very fashionable.
6 Check it ten times first.

29
Pyramid Play

Put the fourteen pictures in order, starting with the shortest pyramid and ending with the tallest.

30
Junior Sudoku

Fill in the grids so each row, column, and 2 x 3 block contains the digits 1–6.

	1			5	6
			1		4
	5			1	
3	2				
		5	4		1
		3			

			6		
	6	4			
6	1		3		5
5				2	
2			4	6	
	3	6	5		

	5	3	2	4	
	1			5	
1	3			2	6
		2	5		
	4			6	

Pond Life

Can you find all the pond life hidden in the grid?

```
Y V Q T W E N I I M I U I M I
E L T A D P O L E M V D U C K
A S F I L Y L F N O G A R D T
G H U Y G E N S L S T I A B O
L S N R A O E E M Q S S R T O
A W R I E M R C A U T D P Y C
H A N U G T T F H I U R L E C
Y N S O S N A E C T R I A O I
L T O E R H E K R O L B V N A
F S R E S L L E S R N W A P S
E O F I T E T G E D A M A B H
N E C E B D N T R H N P S U E
A I E A O T A E P A N O I R R
R B C E I W S O D E E R P N O
C K A T G O L D F I S H E C N
```

ALGAE
BEETLE
BIRD
COOT
CRANEFLY
DRAGONFLY
DUCK
FERN
FROG

GOLDFISH
GOOSE
HERON
LEECH
MAYFLY
MOSQUITO
NEWT
POND SKATER
REED

RUSH
SPAWN
STICKLEBACK
SWAN
TADPOLE
TERRAPIN
VOLE
WATER LILY

32

Quest

All the answers to the clues are four-letter words, and you have to enter them into the grid, starting from the outer squares. When you have done that, you will find a sea creature reading clockwise around the innermost squares starting with number 9.

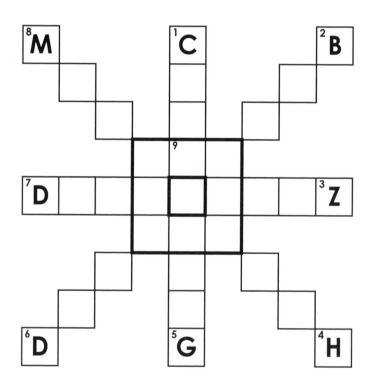

1 Baby lions
2 Water transport
3 Catherine ___-Jones, actress
4 Sixty minutes

5 Tiger Woods' sport
6 Salvador ___, painter
7 Speckles
8 Butterfly-like creature

33

Funny Bones

This clown is on his way home from the circus, but he's forgotten his dog's supper. Can you help him find nine bones hidden in the picture?

34
Kriss Kross

Once you have fitted all the words correctly into the grid, the highlighted letters will spell out something to do with Marigold.

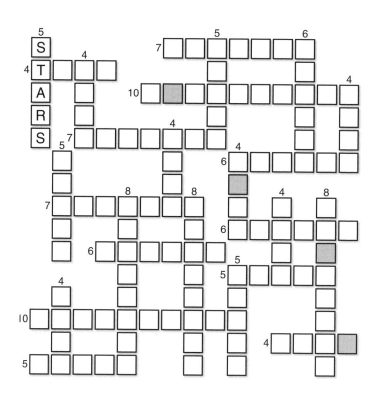

4 letters
COMB
CROP
DARE
GALA
MEAN
PUMA
TUCK
YEAR

5 letters
BIRTH
BLAST
FAIRY
LASSO
RELAX
~~STARS~~

6 letters
BEANIE
CAREER
LOCATE
SUPPLE

7 letters
CURIOUS
PARADOX
STAGGER

8 letters
BIRTHDAY
GEOMETRY
RATIONAL

10 letters
PHILOSOPHY
QUESTIONER

35
Dot to Dot

Join the dots from 1 to 79 to reveal what's going on in the picture.

36
Picture Pairs

Can you find the two identical pictures?

Pick Me Up

Can you decide in what order you
would pick up the twelve paintbrushes
if you could only remove the top
one each time?

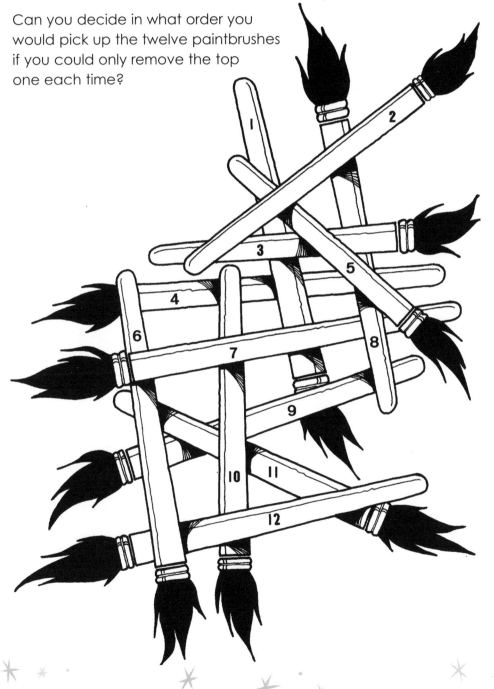

38
Magic Mirror

This mirror is made from lots of small triangular panes of glass.
How many different triangles can you find in the design?

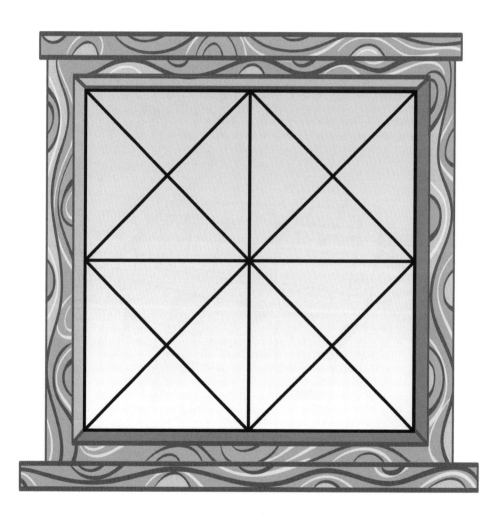

39
Arrowords

Mix with a spoon · Converse about (4,4) · Court procedure · Not genuine · Spring month · Biblical king · Fix · Bread cook

Electrical unit · ___ Stone, *La La Land* star

Jumping insect · Poorly · Uncommon · US coin

Travel on snow · A single time

Animal park · Be untruthful · Climbing aid with rungs

Call a halt to · ___ Ora, singer · Girl's name or part of the eye · Grows older

Chiseled · ___ Smith, *Men in Black* star

Sink your teeth into · Throw up into the air

Get ___ of, discard

Hairless · Cry of regret · Facts and figures · Call for emergency rescue (inits)

Price · Coming from the East · Pleasant melody

Spaghetti, for example · Drop down, like a bird

Heavenly beings · ___ Adams, actress · Vague, hazy · Cook for too long

Beautiful white bird · Grand house

Shut · Large pond · Breadth · Johnny ___, US actor · Hose · Christmas ___, December 24

Aircraft · Up to now

Fruit dessert (5,3) · Sample, taste

Avid, eager · Small snake · Public procession

Jetty, wharf · Large quantity

40
Out of Order

As you can see, the leaf on the right of the stem is growing rapidly. Can you put the eighteen pictures in order, starting with the shortest leaf and ending with the longest?

Suguru & Set Square

Suguru: Each cell in an outlined block must contain a number: A two-cell block contains the numbers 1 and 2; a three-cell block contains the numbers 1, 2, and 3; and so on. The same number must not appear in neighboring cells, not even diagonally.

				4	
			2		3
			3		
4					

Set Square: Place each of the numbers 1–9 in the grid to make the sums work. We've started you with two numbers.

	+		x		= 15
+	■	+	■	-	
	-		+		= 4
+	■	x	■	+	
4	x	8	+		= 35
=		=		=	
12		80		1	

Change a Letter

Solve the clues below, changing one letter of your answer at a time. When you get to clue 12, you'll find that its answer is also one letter different from the first answer—VANE.

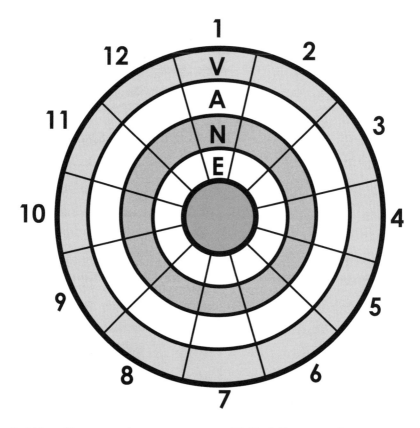

1 Weathercock
2 Grape plant
3 Coal-pit
4 Lion's neck hair
5 Female horse
6 To show bounds or limits
7 Public gardens
8 Actor's role
9 History
10 Final
11 Enormous
12 Container for flowers

43
Nature Trails

Follow each child's trail to discover how they are
planning to spend their afternoon in the woods.

44
Spot the Difference

Can you spot the eight differences?

45

Cross Out

Each of the squares in this grid contains two letters. Can you cross out one letter in each square, so that the remaining letters spell out words in all rows and columns? We've crossed out the T in the top left-hand square to start you off.

T S	O C	O N	O G	S P
P R		W N		W R
C O	H L	L I	V P	E S
R F		O E		S I
A T	O S	T N	G H	G S

Haunted House

There are eight skeleton bones hidden in the picture.
Can you spot them all?

47

Crosswords

Once you have completed the crossword, rearrange the highlighted letters to spell out something to do with Phoebe.

ACROSS
- **1** Idle chatter about others (6)
- **4** Body's digestive canal (7)
- **9** Constellation between Taurus and Pisces (5)
- **10** Showy public display or performance (9)
- **11** (Diseases) that can be caught (10)
- **12** Breeding stable (4)
- **14** Higher of two (5)
- **16** Parts of the feet, sometimes painted (8)
- **18** Bird's plumage (8)
- **21** ___ Claus, Father Christmas (5)
- **23** Final word of a prayer (4)
- **24** Witch's flyer (10)
- **27** Planting and weeding (9)
- **28** Scent, smell (5)
- **29** Horse-seat maker (7)
- **30** Remained in the same place (6)

DOWN
- **1** Kind, courteous (8)
- **2** Rigid, tense (5)
- **3** Feeling of anxiety about the future (10)
- **4** Block of frozen water for cooling drinks (3,4)
- **5** Uses a chair (4)
- **6** Athletics contest comprising ten events (9)
- **7** Firmly fixed, balanced (6)
- **8** Short-sleeved garment (1-5)
- **13** Disallowed beginning of a race (5,5)
- **15** Liked better (9)
- **17** Area behind a house (8)
- **19** At a previous time (7)
- **20** Absorbent item for cleaning dishes (6)
- **22** Giggles (6)
- **25** Elephant tusk substance (5)
- **26** In good health (4)

48
Codeword

In this puzzle, you must decide which letter of the alphabet is represented by each of the numbers 1 to 26. We have already filled in two words, so you can see that A = 6, R = 10, M = 5, Y = 13, and so on. Begin by repeating these letters in each box where their numbers appear in the diagram. You will then have lots of letters to help you start guessing at likely words. All the letters of the alphabet will be used, so as you decide what each one is, cross it off at the side of the grid and enter it in the reference grid at the bottom. The completed grid will look like a filled-in crossword.

1	2	3	2	4		5		6	7	8	9 Z		10	
11		11		2		2	5	7			12 O	13	11	4
14	4	8	5	11	15	2		11	4	16	12 O		16	
17		16		16		15	11	18		11		19	8	20
19	12	15	11	15	12			18		21	11	4	16	2
12			22		14	8	15	23		2		11		22
15	11	22	20	4	2		11		12	18	11	22	20	2
	20		2		11	4	4	12	3		10		2	
20 G	12 O	10 B	4 L	8 I	22 N		12		22	12	12	24	4	2
11		11		24		17	22	2	2		7			11
15	11	16	15	2		11			18	12	15	15	2	18
2	4	17		11		18	7	22		25		2		22
	15		21	4	2	11		2	14	4	8	19	16	2
26	2	18	2			15	11	25		8		2		16
	18		2	24	20	2		15		19	4	2	11	15

Side letters (left): A B C D E F G H I J K L M

Side letters (right): N O P Q R S T U V W X Y Z

1	2	3	4 L	5	6	7	8 I	9 Z	10 B	11	12 O	13
14	15	16	17	18	19	20 G	21	22 N	23	24	25	26

49

Quest

All the answers to the clues are four-letter words, and you have to enter them into the grid, starting from the outer squares. When you have done that, you will discover a type of firework by reading clockwise around the innermost squares starting with number 9.

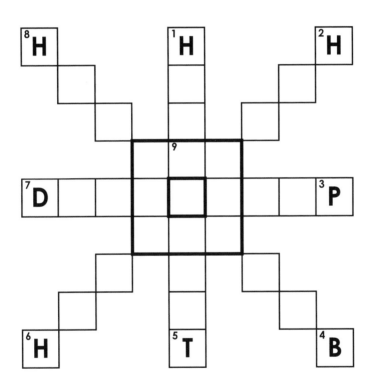

1 Snake's sound
2 Give assistance
3 Italian Leaning Tower city
4 Polar or grizzly animal
5 Chat, speak
6 Back of the foot
7 Numbered cubes
8 Sixty minutes

Camping

Can you find all the words to do with camping hidden in the grid?

```
W  B  A  C  K  P  A  C  K  C  Z  M  O  I  S
R  T  E  E  H  S  D  N  U  O  R  G  U  M  I
A  E  S  T  C  I  A  S  E  U  N  S  T  D  I
A  B  P  G  N  A  H  N  R  N  M  S  D  I  A
F  W  E  E  H  E  N  N  U  T  Y  D  O  S  A
E  O  O  D  L  I  T  V  T  R  E  L  O  P  N
R  A  O  T  R  L  S  E  A  Y  O  I  R  G  E
U  M  E  R  A  O  E  B  N  S  F  D  S  R  N
T  R  H  S  P  H  L  N  O  I  L  U  I  P  E
N  E  I  O  S  R  R  L  T  D  A  F  I  Z  P
E  T  L  Y  V  E  E  T  K  E  P  T  I  A  O
V  P  L  L  T  N  O  T  C  M  C  P  E  I  R
D  F  E  N  A  R  R  I  A  H  S  E  R  F  Y
A  S  A  G  C  M  O  C  B  W  L  I  L  O  U
A  L  T  H  S  L  E  E  P  I  N  G  B  A  G
```

ADVENTURE	FRESH AIR	POLE
BACKPACK	GROUNDSHEET	REPELLENT
BACK-TO-NATURE	GUY ROPE	SHELTER
BEDROLL	LANTERN	SLEEPING BAG
CAMPFIRE	MALLET	TENT
CANVAS	OUTDOORS	TORCH
COUNTRYSIDE	PEG	WATERPROOF
FLAP	PITCH	ZIP
FLY SHEET		

51

Magic Boxes

In a magic box, the words read the same across
and down, as in the sample below.

Make three more magic boxes using the words listed below
and make sure that the word POLE appears in each box.

R	O	M	P
O	H	I	O
M	I	L	L
P	O	L	E

LOOT	STEW	POLE
ALTO	OVEN	ALPS
LEND	NEON	SPAN
POLE	POLE	ENDS

52
Pick Me Up

Can you decide in what order you would pick up the thirteen pens if you could only remove the top one each time?

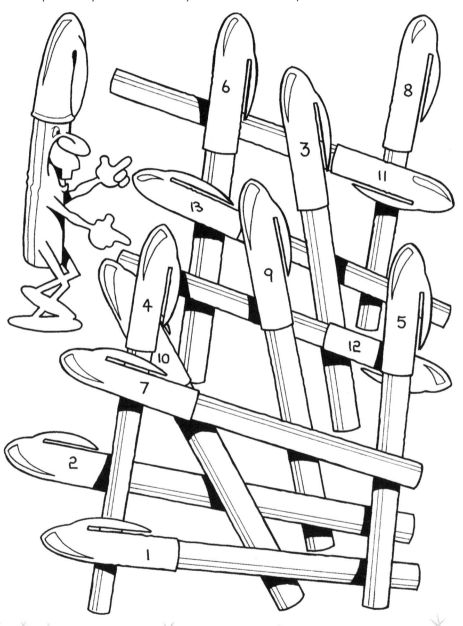

53
Kriss Kross

Once you have fitted all the words correctly into the grid, the highlighted letters will spell out something to do with how Phoebe and Marigold became friends.

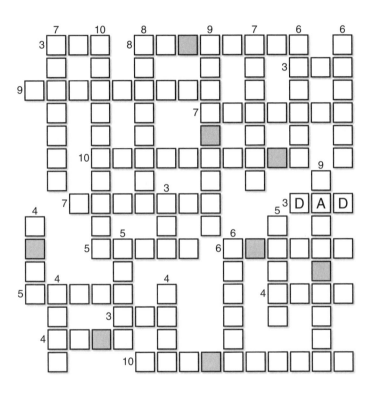

3 letters
~~DAD~~
ERR
HOW
PEP
TOM

4 letters
DISC
LARK
LAZY
TRAY
ZANY

5 letters
ABBEY
CLIMB
FILLY

YAPPY

6 letters
EDIBLE
EXHALE
THRUSH
TWELVE

7 letters
CALYPSO
ENTENTE
TURBINE
UNEQUAL

8 letters
DEADBEAT
DELIVERY

9 letters
BALLERINA
DEDUCTION
GRASSLAND

10 letters
HYSTERICAL
MISSIONARY
OVERSTITCH

Count on Me

How many teddies can you find in this jumbled heap?

55
Dot to Dot

Join the dots from 1 to 176 to reveal what's going on in the picture.

56
Number jig

Fit all the listed series of numbers into the grid.

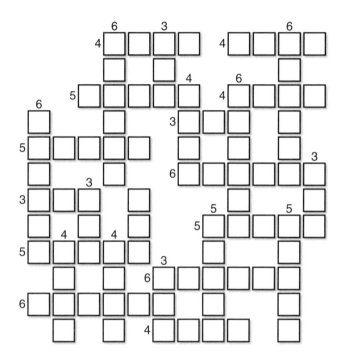

3 digits	4 digits	5 digits	6 digits
177	2438	12113	111256
224	3275	44547	333312
304	3634	81307	338817
363	4217	83275	345615
402	4820	86184	614604
575	8388	95049	714872
675	9417		823416

Change a Letter

Solve the clues below, in order, changing one letter of your answer each time to make a new word to fit the next clue. When you get round to clue 12, you will find that its answer is just one letter different from the first answer—COPE.

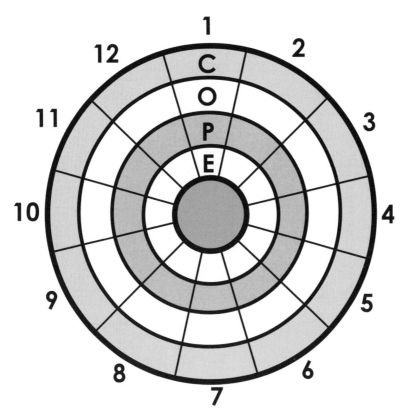

1 ~~Manage~~
2 Cloak
3 Small restaurant
4 Item of luggage
5 Money
6 List of actors in a film
7 Price
8 Mail
9 Sit for an artist
10 Flower
11 Watering pipe
12 Wish for

58
Junior Sudoku

Fill in the grids so each row, column, and 2 x 3 block contains the digits 1–6.

	4		1		
		2	5	6	
6		5		1	2
			6	3	
					6
			3		

	3	2	4	5	
	2	6	5	1	
2					1
4	1			2	5

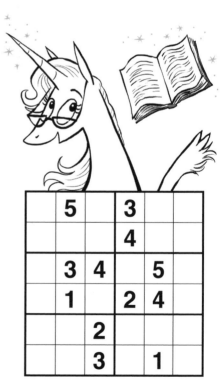

	5		3		
			4		
	3	4		5	
	1		2	4	
		2			
		3		1	

Suguru & Set Square

Suguru: Each cell in an outlined block must contain a number: A two-cell block contains the numbers 1 and 2; a three-cell block contains the numbers 1, 2, and 3; and so on. The same number must not appear in neighboring cells, not even diagonally.

		3			**2**
2			**2**		

Set Square: Place each of the numbers 1–9 in the grid to make the sums work. We've started you with two numbers.

4	+		x		= 108
x		x		÷	
	-		÷		= 4
+		+		-	
5	x		-		= 4
=		=		=	
33		26		3	

60
Picture Pairs

Can you find the two identical pictures?

Easter Egg Hunt

Can you find a path through the maze to help Phoebe get to her Easter egg?

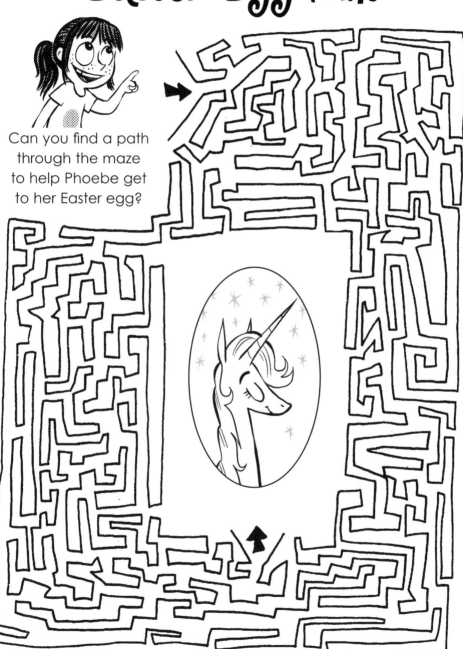

62
Square Pair

There are six pairs of identical squares in the scene below. Can you work out which ones they are?

	A.	B.	C.	D.	E.	F.	G.
1.							
2.							
3.							
4.							
5.							
6.							
7.							
8.							
9.							

63
Hot Stuff

Sir Egbert is having a barbecue with the help of his friend Douglas. Can you find eight sausages hidden in the picture?

Quest

All the answers to the clues below are four-letter words, and you
have to enter them in the grid starting from the outer squares.
If you do so correctly, a way of getting into buildings
will be revealed starting with number 9.

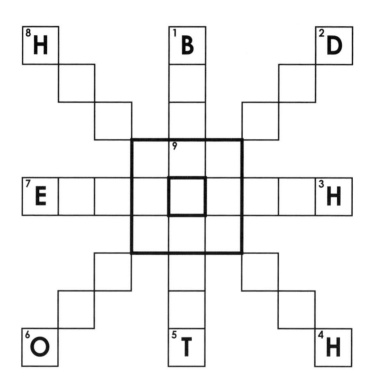

1 Two-wheeled vehicle   6 Not closed
2 Break of day   7 Long poem or story
3 Injured   8 Very large
4 Sixty minutes
5 Large fish

65

Spot the Difference

Can you spot the eight differences?

66

Pick Me Up

Can you decide in what order you would pick up the eleven rulers if you could only remove the top one each time?

67
Crosswords

Once you have completed the crossword, rearrange the highlighted letters to spell out something to do with how Phoebe and Marigold became friends.

ACROSS
1 Game played on ice or grass (6)
4 Film about heroic events (4)
7 Long-bodied public vehicle (3)
10 Half-year school terms (9)
11 Revolving part of a helicopter (5)
12 Opposite of "succeeded" (6)
13 Bead of liquid (7)
15 Flowers with thorns (5)
17 Goes farther in the same direction (7,2)
20 Ongoing TV series about a group of characters (4,5)
22 Not old (5)
24 Take part in a religious ceremony (7)
26 Forgetful, disorganized (6)
29 Hard yellowish resin, used in jewelry (5)
30 Sensitive topic (4,5)
31 Have a meal (3)
32 Periods of 24 hours (4)
33 Field of grassland (6)

DOWN
1 Make a noise like a snake (4)
2 North-showing device (7)
3 Painter's picture support (5)
5 Sat for a photograph (5)
6 Desire to know or learn (9)
7 Glass containers (7)
8 Walk swaggeringly (5)
9 Pain in the skull area (8)
14 Upper limbs (4)
16 Suffocated (9)
18 Give comfort to (8)
19 ___ area, danger zone (2-2)
21 Circus gymnast (7)
23 Not yet attempted (7)
24 Produce cloth on a loom (5)
25 Brash and domineering (5)
27 Plentiful (5)
28 Pack away (in an aircraft's overhead bin) (4)

68
Out of Order

Can you put the fourteen pictures in order, starting with the shortest drip of paint and ending with the longest?

Suguru & Set Square

Suguru: Each cell in an outlined block must contain a number: A two-cell block contains the numbers 1 and 2; a three-cell block contains the numbers 1, 2, and 3; and so on. The same number must not appear in neighboring cells, not even diagonally.

				4	
		5			
					4
		4		3	

Set Square: Place each of the numbers 1–9 in the grid to make the sums work. We've started you with two numbers.

6	x		-	= 33
+	■	+	■	+
	-		x	= 12
+	■	-	■	-
	-	2	x	= 16
= 15		= 6		= 4

Strictly Ballroom

The twenty moves that make up the Random Fandango are pictured below.

The number on each footprint indicates how many moves to make, while the letters provide the direction (D for Down, U for Up, L for Left, and R for Right).

If the "black star" step is the last move to make, which is the first?

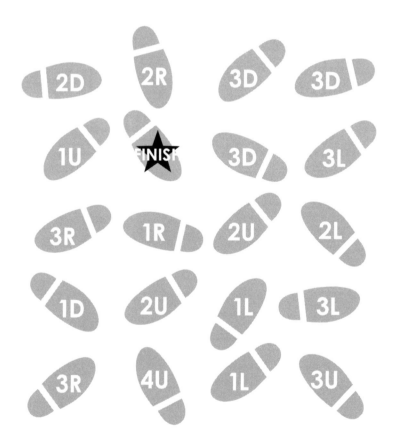

Cross Out

Each of the squares in this crossword grid contains two letters. Can you cross out one letter in each square, so that the remaining letters spell out words in all rows and columns? We've crossed out the P in the top left-hand square to start you off.

P̶ C	P R	E A	A S	R M
L O		G A		O E
L A	F N	G R	Y E	L U
S O		L O		G O
N S	I T	E N	T R	N H

72

Kriss Kross

Once you have fitted all the words correctly into the grid, the highlighted letters will spell out something to do with Marigold.

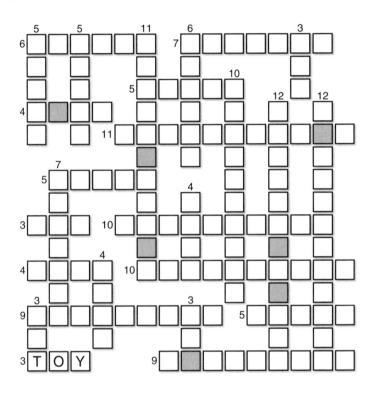

3 letters
EGO
FRY
HOT
MEN
~~TOY~~

4 letters
FANG
GLEN
LAMB
SUCH

5 letters
ADMIT
BRASS
HOIST
KNOCK
TOAST

6 letters
BIKINI
THIRST

7 letters
THICKEN
TORNADO

9 letters
ENCOURAGE
HONEYCOMB

10 letters
EMBLEMATIC
TIMEKEEPER
UNSALEABLE

11 letters
DRESSMAKING
INHERITANCE

12 letters
SKATEBOARDER
UNAPPETIZING

Magic Marigold

Can you find all the words to do with Marigold hidden in the grid?

```
B K W T C J E S E N A M Z X D
I N A I S H P Y F S T E B I T
Y I G D C L L R I P O L D T I
L A H A E N I U O E C E L D R
M V N N E E J R T L I G O B M
S A D V N K O E T L R A G T I
P O A D E W H Y A S U N I E C
R E U N I C O R N L O T R D S
H S L U F E C A R G O N A R A
T S P O I T E N A R S U M E O
I E E A T G M A B F E B S C D
Z N X V R L E G W A R M E R S
A I N T O K R H Y T U A E B S
P F U I S O L O T E P A C L N
R H O R N E H E I S O A T S Y
```

BEAUTY
ELEGANT
FINESSE
FRIEND
GRACEFUL
HEAVENLY
HOOVES
HORN

JEALOUS
LEG WARMERS
MAGIC
MANE
MARIGOLD
NOSTRILS
PANACHE
SCARF

SPARKLE
SPELLS
SPLENDOR
TAIL
TEXTS
UNICORN
VAIN
ZAP

Change a Letter

Solve the clues below, in order, changing one letter of your answer each time to make a new word to fit the next clue. When you get round to clue 12, you will find that its answer is just one letter different from the first answer—FARM.

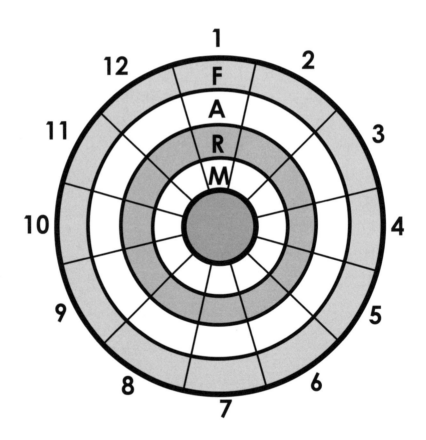

1 Land for growing crops
2 Not cold
3 Lump on the skin
4 Piece
5 Not future or present
6 Huge

7 Quick
8 Not fiction
9 Front part of the head
10 Price to travel on a bus
11 Shoot a gun
12 Solid, not soft

75
Number jig

Fit all the listed series of numbers into the grid.

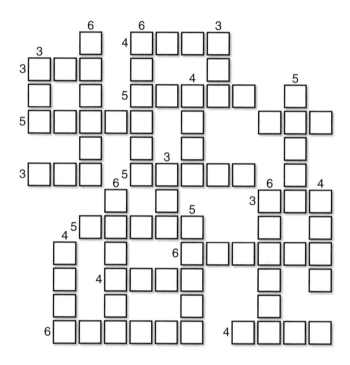

3 digits	4 digits	5 digits	6 digits
185	1305	26880	572770
245	5217	38775	664712
282	6258	45970	687058
658	7888	55562	705302
692	8202	56517	772135
887	9118	57325	923512
932			

76
Shed Some Light

Professor Crackpot hasn't realized that his robot isn't plugged in. Can you help shed a little light on the situation by finding the eight small lightbulbs that are hidden in the picture?

77

Codeword

In this puzzle, you must decide which letter of the alphabet is represented by each of the numbers 1 to 26. We have already filled in two words, so you can see that A = 6, R = 10, M = 5, Y = 13, and so on. Begin by repeating these letters in each box where their numbers appear in the diagram. You will then have lots of letters to help you start guessing at likely words. All the letters of the alphabet will be used, so as you decide what each one is, cross it off at the side of the grid and enter it in the reference grid at the bottom. The completed grid will look like a filled-in crossword.

23	10	6	17	8		11		20	3	25	4			2	
6		14		16		9	5	3			16	15	9	21	
14	9	10	11	3	5	9		6	5	5	16		17		
25		16		24		18	6	10		6		11	9	17	
18	6	21	19	9	5			10	9	14	18	25	8	9	
6			16		6	10	5	13		8		12		10	
8	6	19	19	9	10		6		19	9	8	9	18	9	
	25		7		10	6	19	25	16		13		9		
26	10	9	9	4	13		6		3	21	10	9	6	8	
9		6		9		24	5	3	7		25			6	
6	23	10	16	26	6	18			22	16	23	1	9	13	
19	9	21		10		6	7	16		6		21		9	
	8		1	6	10	18		5	25	24	22	9	6	10	
26	8	3	9			3	24	9		25		9		9	
	16		13	3	8	9		21		24	6	8	6	19	

Letters down the left: A B C D E F G H I J K L M
Letters down the right: N O P Q R S T U V W X Y Z

Filled-in words: A R M Y (6 10 5 13), H O C K E Y (22 16 23 1 9 13)

1	2	3	4	5	6	7	8	9	10	11	12	13
K				M	A			E	R			Y
14	15	16	17	18	19	20	21	22	23	24	25	26
		O						H	C			

junior Sudoku

Fill in the grids so each row, column, and 2 x 3 block contains the digits 1–6.

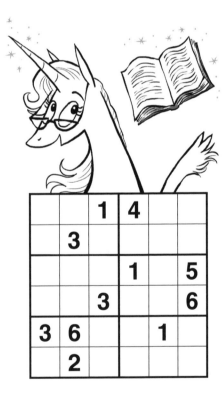

Sinking Feeling

Can you help Phoebe through the
maze to get to her inner tube?

80

Quest

All the answers to the clues are four-letter words, and you have to enter them into the grid, starting from the outer squares. When you have done that, you will find some fun vehicle reading clockwise around the innermost squares starting with number 9.

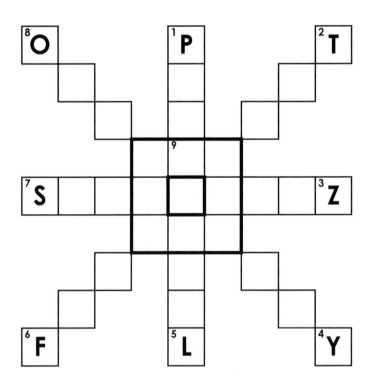

1 Writing tools

2 White powder for the body

3 Nil, nothing

4 Stringed toy (2-2)

5 Opposite of first

6 Number of legs on a starfish

7 Twinkling feature of the night sky

8 Messenger birds in the Harry Potter books

81
Dot to Dot

Join the dots from 1 to 124 to reveal what's going on in the picture.

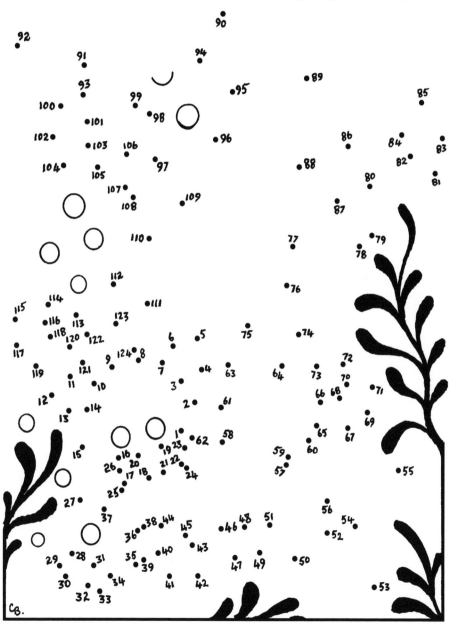

82
Picture Pairs

Can you find the two identical pictures?

83
Cross Out

Each of the squares in this grid contains two letters. Can you cross out one letter in each square so the remaining letters spell out words in all rows and columns? We've crossed out the L in the top left-hand square to start you off.

L M	O U	W S	I E	S C
O A		N T		K H
G N	A L	O I	F V	E R
G I		R L		O S
Y C	O I	B M	C E	T B

Sweet Success

Poor Oscar is quaking at the thought of a kiss from Glenda Grotbreath. Only his sweets will save him now! Can you help him find all ten of them before Glenda puckers up?

85
Spot the Difference

Can you spot the eight differences?

Hidden Words

There are imaginary beings hidden among the letters of the sentences below. Can you spot all six?

1 To play this game you go blindfolded around the room.
2 Put the red rag on the table.
3 In the summer, maids are employed at holiday camps.
4 It's the yellow tunic or nothing.
5 Night patrol left the soldier feeling tired.
6 My neighbor has a teenage niece.

Crosswords

Once you have completed the crossword, rearrange the highlighted letters to spell out something to do with Marigold.

ACROSS

1 Become invisible (6)
4 Remove the packaging from (6)
10 Set of channels available via distribution lines (5,10)
11 Medical care (9)
12 Hurriedness (5)
13 Chicago airport (5)
15 Entrance to the cellar via a hole set in the floor above (8)
19 Someone who doesn't belong to a group (8)
20 Mid-sentence punctuation mark (5)
22 Junior soldier (5)
24 Comic-book good guy (9)
26 Expression of good wishes (15)
27 Shoelace's hole (6)
28 Clever, intelligent (6)

DOWN

1 Trip (8)
2 High-born, lordly (5)
3 Sugary quality (9)
5 High-pitched cry of a horse (5)
6 Sudden heavy shower (9)
7 Breathed heavily (6)
8 Carefully chosen (8)
9 Of the highest quality (4)
14 Plentiful supply (9)
16 All of a sudden, without warning (8)
17 Person who paints and wallpapers (9)
18 In a way that is well known (8)
21 Frozen spike of water (6)
23 "___ Blind Mice", nursery song (5)
24 Building plot (4)
25 Expressive image or icon (in text messages) (5)

Suguru & Set Square

Suguru: Each cell in an outlined block must contain a number: A two-cell block contains the numbers 1 and 2; a three-cell block contains the numbers 1, 2, and 3; and so on. The same number must not appear in neighboring cells, not even diagonally.

			4		
					2
		5			
				4	
				3	

Set Square: Place each of the numbers 1–9 in the grid to make the sums work. We've started you with two numbers.

	x	6	÷		= 3
-	■	÷	■	-	
	+		x		= 20
+	■	+	■	+	
2	x		+		= 23
= 5		= 9		= 12	

Magic Boxes

In a magic box, the words read the same across
and down, as in the sample below.

Make three more magic boxes using the words listed below
and make sure that the word NONE appears in each box.

M	I	N	T
I	V	O	R
N	O	N	E
T	R	E	K

NONE	ENDS	OVEN
NEED	KNIT	HALO
INKS	TEST	THAN
ALAN	NONE	NONE

90
Pick Me Up

Can you decide in what order you would pick up the twelve pencils if you could only take the top one each time?

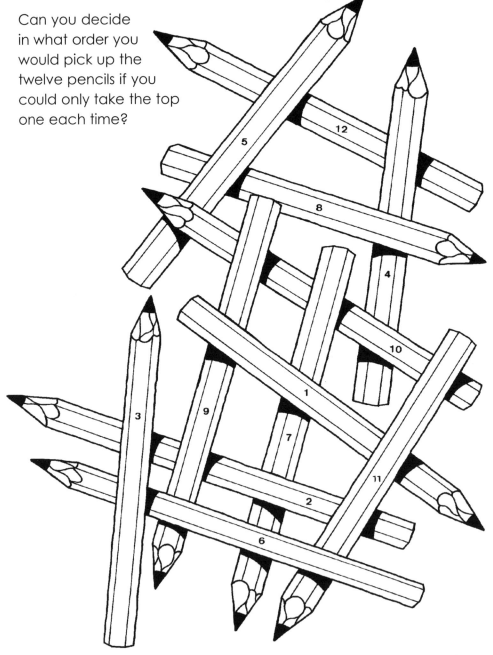

91
Kriss Kross

Once you have fitted all the words correctly into the grid, the highlighted letters will spell out a character from *Phoebe and Her Unicorn*.

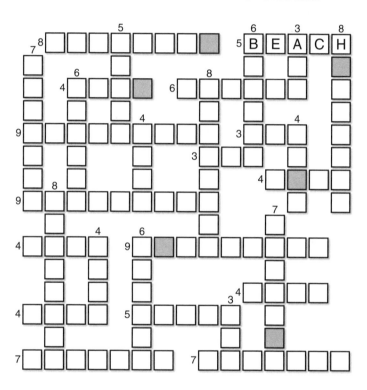

3 letters
ART
HIM
ICE
LIP

4 letters
ACME
COMB
FLEA
HUNT

PALE
PULP
RAMP
STOP

5 letters
BEACH
CLOTH
COMET

6 letters
BEETLE
COMMON
MUSCLE
OBJECT

7 letters
ASHAMED
CHICANE
EMPEROR
PLASTIC

8 letters
BEGINNER
HOSPITAL
OUTCLASS
STICKING

9 letters
CONDITION
MICROCHIP
SOMETHING

92

Square Pairs

Can you find six pairs of matching squares in the picture below?

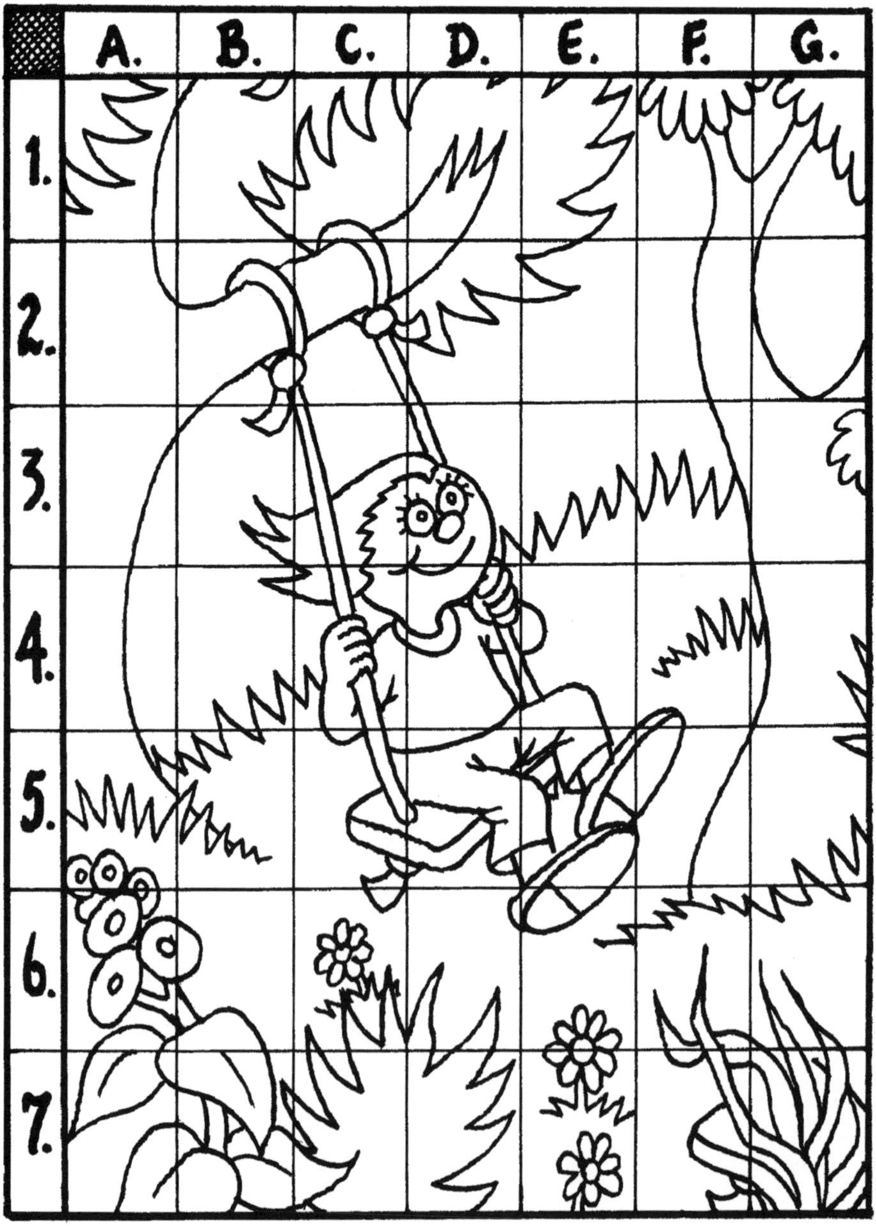
A.
B.
C.
D.
E.
F.
G.
1.
2.
3.
4.
5.
6.
7.

93
Change a Letter

Solve the clues below, in order, changing one letter of your answer each time to make a new word to fit the next clue. When you get round to clue 12, you will find that its answer is just one letter different from the first answer—CAPE.

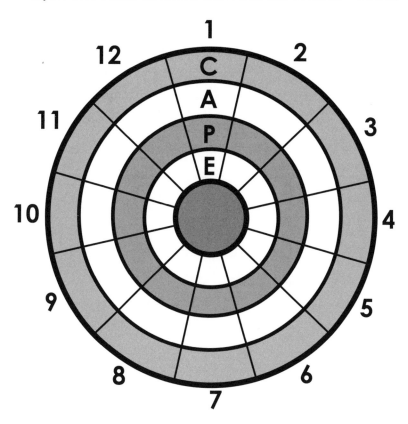

1 ~~Batman's cloak~~
2 Hamster's enclosure
3 Item of luggage
4 Group of actors
5 Quick
6 Clenched hand
7 Shopping ___, note of things to buy
8 Final one
9 History, time gone
10 Actor's role
11 Horse and ___, old transport
12 Mind, be concerned

Number Jig

Fit all the listed series of numbers into the grid.

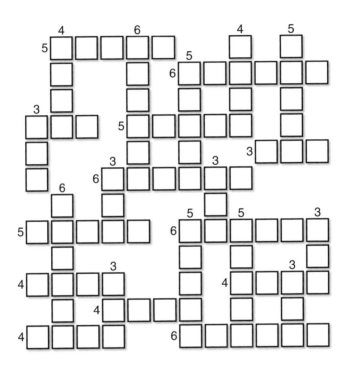

3 digits	4 digits	5 digits	6 digits
124	2263	13171	423280
133	4172	28352	517246
364	5312	30667	577505
372	6679	55435	653401
507	7632	66317	700767
667	9737	74844	836631
787		76967	
922			

95

Quest

All the answers to the clues are four-letter words, and you have to enter them into the grid, starting from the outer squares. When you have done that, you will find something connected with travel reading clockwise around the innermost squares starting with number 9.

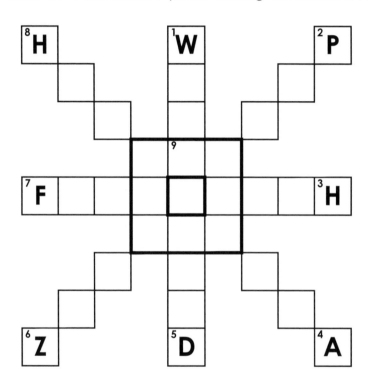

1 Stinging insect

2 Large wild American cat

3 Snake's sound

4 Swiss mountain range

5 Slightly wet

6 Nil, none

7 Number of sides of a square

8 Warmth

Picture Pairs

Can you find the two identical pictures?

junior Sudoku

Fill in the grids so each row, column, and 2 x 3 block contains the digits 1–6.

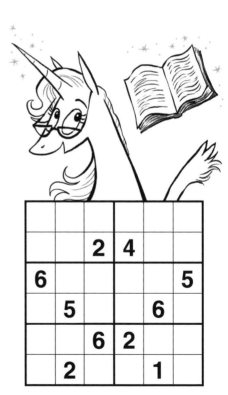

Cross Out

Each of the squares in this crossword grid contains two letters. Can you cross out one letter in each square so the remaining letters spell out words in all rows and columns? We've crossed out the P in the top left-hand square to start you off.

P̷/F	I/L	A/R	G/S	T/Y
L/U		F/A		I/A
K/A	S/L	I/O	N/E	N/T
D/M		S/Y		L/G
E/S	N/R	L/E	M/W	D/Y

99
Sparkle

Can you find all the words that mean "sparkle" hidden in the grid?

```
D A Z Z L E E Y H S A L F E O
O O D O S A S L O G P Y D C V
G E S H O R N Y K A L B E N I
S L I E H O T I Z R R O P A B
C N I S R I D R M I A A W I R
E B A T L E E M L A N P S D A
O D R A T T M L E A T P S A N
W H T N W E I M C Y M I V R T
Z I N G I A R H I A E C O D S
V R O T N E E E E H N R T N S
E O T C K L O L G M S F N B E
C Z E D L A G I R E K C I L F
N Z R H E N S O R T E P L A N
R I T I R I P S E B S O G A T
Y F S C I N T I L L A T E E C
```

ANIMATION
BRILLIANCE
BRIO
DASH
DAZZLE
ELAN
FIZZ
FLASH
FLICKER

GLEAM
GLINT
GLITTER
GLOW
PANACHE
RADIANCE
SCINTILLATE
SHIMMER
SHINE

SPARKLE
SPIRIT
TWINKLE
VIBRANT
VIM
VITALITY
ZAP
ZING

100
Spot the Difference

Can you spot the eight differences?

101
Name Game

Complete the answers to the clues, then take the missing letters, in order, to find out what you get if you feed ducks with gunpowder.

1 Workplace   O F _ _ C E
2 Breakfast food   C E _ _ A L
3 Imaginary line around the Earth   E _ _ A T O R
4 Small meals   S N _ _ K S
5 Bread and cakes shop   B A _ _ R Y
6 Human being   P E _ _ O N

102
Splitz

The answers to these clues have been split in two and placed in the jumbled heap. Can you solve the clues and put the split words back together? Write your answers in the grid and transfer the coded letters to the smaller grid. If you do so correctly, you will discover a type of flavoring.

	A	B	C	D	E	F
1						
2	E	R	A	S	E	D
3						
4						
5						
6						

3E	1D	2B	6F	4D	6B

SCH   ORA   ~~SED~~   ING   NGE   SMO

ACT   ANA   OTH   ~~ERA~~   OOL   BAN

1 Yellow fruit
2 Rubbed out
3 A fruit or color
4 Working in the theater or on film
5 Not rough
6 Place of learning

103
Mountain Maze

These climbers need to scale the rock face starting at the arrow and climb back down again without straying into the path of the mountain goat. Can you steer them safely through?

DOWN...

104
Count on Me

Can you figure out how many shoes
there are in the jumbled heap?

105
Codeword

In this puzzle, you must decide which letter of the alphabet is represented by each of the numbers 1 to 26. We have already filled in two words, so you can see that S = 4, Q = 12, U = 26, A = 17, D = 15, and so on. Begin by repeating these letters in each box where their numbers appear in the diagram. You will then have lots of letters to help you start guessing at likely words. All the letters of the alphabet will be used, so as you decide what each one is, cross it off at the side of the grid and enter it in the reference grid at the bottom. The completed grid will look like a filled-in crossword.

20	25	17	4	6		1		14	17	1	10		7	
17		25		21		10	14	26			11	22	21	5
6	13	17	4	6	10	22		8	25	17	11		24	
2		22		25		13	8 O	8 F		19		9	10	6
6	21	14	20	10	22			21		17	25	13	5	10
26			25		2	13	22	5		3		21		25
20	17	3	10	22	23		17		3	10	5	5	10	25
	11		10		14	13	6	6	13		17		17	
6	13	18	18	25	10		21		17	20	4	13	22	20
10		25		10		6	13	13	25		6			22
4	12	26	17	15		2			17	5	23	13	5	10
6	26	11		11		21	5	3		21		16		17
	17		15	10	17	22		5	10	11	25	10	16	6
17	16	2	10			4	3	21		2		17		2
	3		5	10	19	6		6		6	10	5	4	10

A
B
C
D
E
F
G
H
I
J S Q U A D
K
L
M

N
O̶
P
Q̶
R
S̶
T
U̶
V
W
X
Y
Z

| 1 | 2 | 3 | 4 S | 5 | 6 | 7 | 8 F | 9 | 10 | 11 | 12 Q | 13 O |
| 14 | 15 D | 16 | 17 A | 18 | 19 | 20 | 21 | 22 | 23 | 24 | 25 | 26 U |

106
Strictly Ballroom

The twenty moves that make up the Random Fandango are pictured below.

The number on each footprint indicates how many moves to make, while the letters provide the direction (D for Down, U for Up, L for Left, and R for Right).

If the "black star" step is the last move to make, which is the first?

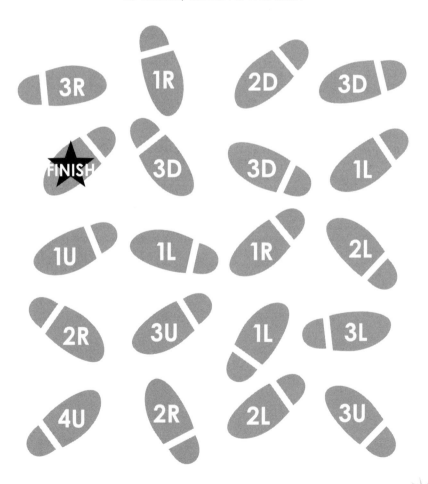

Dot to dot

Join the dots from 1 to 96 to reveal the hidden picture.

108
Square Pairs

There are six pairs of identical squares in the underwater scene below. How quickly can you spot them?

Magic Boxes

In a magic box, the words read the same across and down, as in the sample below.

Make three more magic boxes using the words listed below and make sure that the word ECHO appears in each box.

T	A	M	E
A	L	E	C
M	E	S	H
E	C	H	O

CROP	SHOW	OPEN
ECHO	HOSE	WREN
PEST	ECHO	TOWN
NEON	RICE	ECHO

110

Feeling Fruity

There are ten bananas hidden in the scene below. Can you find them all?

Hidden Words

Hidden in each of the sentences below is a word related to trees. Can you find all six?

1 The first run Kitty took part in was a success.
2 The falcon, eagle, and hawk are birds of prey.
3 Bob ran charity events for local good causes.
4 Is a bobble a fancy decoration on a hat?
5 My best wig is a blonde one.
6 Good boots will last umpteen years.

Splitz

The answers to these clues have been split in two and placed in the jumbled heap. Can you solve the clues and put the split words back together? Write your answers in the grid and transfer the coded letters to the smaller grid. If you do so correctly, you will discover a type of bird.

	A	B	C	D	E	F
1						
2						
3						
4	S	U	N	S	E	T
5						
6						

2F	6B	5D	3C	1D	4E

HEM   PET   MAY   NOT   PEP   GET

~~SUN~~   ICE   PER   CAR   ~~SET~~   FOR

1 Spot something
2 Absolute chaos
3 Salt and ___, seasoning
4 ~~Dusk~~
5 Opposite of remember
6 Floor-covering

113
Out of Order

Put the eighteen pictures in order, starting with number 11, which is twenty past twelve, and working your way through the day from there. Be careful, it's quite tricky.

Name Game

Solve the clues and fill in the missing letters in the spaces provided. Then take the missing letters, in order, to find out what's soft, sweet, and fluffy and comes from Mars.

1 ___ sauce, ketchup   T O _ _ T O

2 Hospital workers   N U _ _ E S

3 Girl or woman   F E _ _ L E

4 Color of an egg yolk   Y E _ _ O W

5 Daffodil or rose, for example   F L _ _ E R

115

Which Way Out?

Can you help Marigold find her way to the exit?

116
Square Pairs

There are six pairs of identical squares in the scene below.
Can you find them all?

117
Splitz

The answers to these clues have been split in two and placed in the jumbled heap. Can you solve the clues and put the split words back together? Write your answers in the grid and transfer the coded letters to the smaller grid. If you have done this correctly, something you should try to be will be spelled out.

	A	B	C	D	E	F
1						
2						
3						
4						
5	N	O	T	I	C	E
6						

3D	5B	2F	1B	6D	2D

SUN   USE   ICE   SHY   FAT   REF

ZIP   TAN   HER   NOT   MAR   PER

1 Say no
2 Bronzed skin
3 Male parent
4 Toothed fastener on jeans
5 Spot, see
6 Boggy

118

Count Up

How many eggs has this chicken laid?

Hidden Words

There is an item of clothing hidden among the words of each of the sentences below. Can you find all five?

1 Freddie was naughty, so Annabel told him off.
2 Doing the flamenco at the dance was great fun.
3 On the first day of the semester, sombre rows of children stood in the hall.
4 Serious car fanatics went to the Auto Show every day.
5 Keep on chopping the vegetables for dinner.

120
Shade It

Color in each fragment of this picture that
contains one dot to reveal a hidden picture.

121
Sail Away

It's approaching sunset and the yacht is gradually enveloped in shade. Put the eighteen pictures in order, starting with the unshaded yacht and ending with the one that is completely darkened.

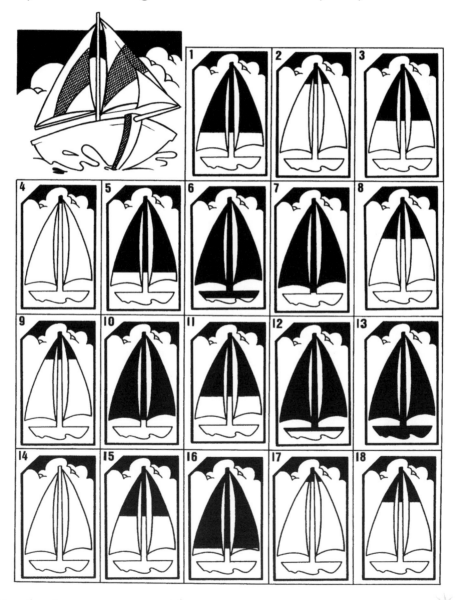

Solutions

1. KRISS KROSS

```
GRIP HUT DEDUCE
E   H   I O   A
OFFICER GOVERN
O   U   E     A
ARC DESK N E V A
M   C   O I T A A
FARO ELEVATION
T   Q   V   R L
 MULBERRY   ITS
 E   D I    O
NEATER ATTACHE
U  T  J U L O P
BASIC I A L USE
C  S  BULBOUS A K
E  HAKE   W  E  K
```

DAKOTA

2. QUEST

1 Chip 2 Puma 3 Jeep 4 Blue
5 Hour 6 Rich 7 Flea 8 Exit
9 PAPER HAT

3. TONY'S PANTS

Path 2

4. SPOT THE DIFFERENCE

5. NUMBER JIG

```
1     9 0 8 0 6 7   2
7 6 2 4 3   3     6   6
4   5   4   3 1 5 7 7 6
3 0 1   4 1 7     5
    1 6 5     3 8 9 6
3   8       5   2
3 5 2   5   9 0   8
7     4 7 6 8 4   1   1
5 3 6   2   7   9 8 2 1 6
  5   9 1 0 0   1   6
8 5 8 5 4   4     8
  0   7 7 2 0 5 3
```

6. SUGURU

```
1 3 2 1 2 1
2 4 5 3 5 3
5 1 2 4 2 4
3 4 3 1 3 1
1 2 5 4 5 2
4 3 1 2 1 3
```

6. SET SQUARE

4	x	5	÷	2
x	■	x	■	+
3	x	6	x	1
+	■	+	■	x
9	x	7	x	8

Solutions

7. CROSSWORDS

H	E	A	P		S	P	E	C	T	A	C	L	E	S
O		D		B		E		O		L		A		W
M	O	V	I	E		R	E	I	N	F	O	R	C	E
E		E		H		C		N		A		G		D
P	E	N	T	A	G	O	N		F	L	E	E	C	E
A		T		V		L		T		F				N
G	A	U	Z	E		A	N	I	M	A	T	O	R	
E		R				T		M			B		R	
	H	E	R	M	I	O	N	E		T	H	E	M	E
H			E		R		W		I		D		S	
E	X	C	E	S	S		C	A	M	P	S	I	T	E
D		H		S		L		S		T		E		A
G	U	I	T	A	R	I	S	T		O	W	N	E	R
E		N		G		M		E		E		C		C
S	K	A	T	E	B	O	A	R	D		M	E	S	H

HOWELL

8. CHANGE A LETTER

1 Pale **2** Tale **3** Talk **4** Walk
5 Wall **6** Ball **7** Bell **8** Cell
9 Tell **10** Till **11** Pill **12** Pile

9. MYTHICAL CREATURES

A	R	E	M	I	H	C	D	I	A	M	R	E	M	D
T	S	T	D	S	T	S	B	E	P	I	Y	N	U	B
A	T	K	R	A	K	E	N	A	T	C	D	A	S	E
O	T	U	Q	E	A	W	S	O	S	C	D	L	M
T	X	A	L	G	S	E	O	T	A	I	R	F	E	O
N	N	P	W	H	R	R	Y	U	E	C	L	P	D	N
L	I	L	E	P	R	E	C	H	A	U	N	I	S	G
E	H	L	S	A	O	W	T	P	M	I	E	N	S	U
C	P	A	M	S	E	O	O	L	L	E	T	N	N	K
E	S	H	G	E	T	L	A	B	E	B	O	I	I	E
N	Y	C	O	R	R	F	O	H	D	G	C	N	F	P
T	R	R	O	E	H	G	S	S	A	O	U	O	F	I
A	T	L	I	E	N	N	A	R	R	Y	E	T	I	X
U	L	L	N	A	A	I	D	N	R	E	I	S	R	I
R	O	A	T	B	F	Y	X	E	C	D	L	R	G	E

10. CROSS OUT

```
T  R  A  I  N
O     D     U
R  I  D  E  R
C     E     S
H  O  R  S  E
```

11. JUNIOR SUDOKU

3	4	5	6	2	1
2	1	6	5	4	3
1	5	2	3	6	4
6	3	4	2	1	5
4	6	3	1	5	2
5	2	1	4	3	6

4	3	6	5	2	1
5	1	2	4	6	3
2	4	1	3	5	6
6	5	3	1	4	2
3	2	5	6	1	4
1	6	4	2	3	5

2	6	1	4	3	5
3	5	4	6	1	2
5	3	2	1	6	4
4	1	6	5	2	3
6	2	5	3	4	1
1	4	3	2	5	6

12. PICTURE PAIRS
2 and 3 are the same.

13. COUNT UP
There are sixteen bats.

14. DOT TO DOT
It's a dragon.

Solutions

15. KRISS KROSS

```
COLD     SCAFFOLD
A  U     I    D  R  A
BACKHAND  D    D  E  DEW
 B  E NER  R    I  N
 A    MOUSSE  INK
USE  T    S    A  G
 H    CHORISTER  A
 E    E U  E    YES  S
 DECOR  SWEEP    S  Y
  O    H    E  Y
 DRUDGE    AIRER
 O N A    L  T  O
 W  D  TUG  ADJUST
 STOVE  U    E  R  E
 E    INSCRIBE
```
POND

16. PICK ME UP
11, 2, 13, 6, 4, 12, 5, 8, 1,
10, 14, 7, 3, 9

17. QUEST
1 Lamb **2** Lisa **3** Wall **4** Foal
5 Poor **6** Polo **7** *Nemo*
8 Term **9** BALLROOM

18. STRICTLY BALLROOM

19. MAGIC BOXES

LATE	SLAM	PILL
AXEL	LATE	IDEA
TEAM	ATOM	LEFT
ELMS	MEMO	LATE

20. SUGURU

3	4	1	2	1	4
1	2	3	5	3	2
4	5	1	2	1	5
1	3	4	5	3	2
2	5	2	1	4	1
1	3	4	3	2	5

20. SET SQUARE

5	x	3	+	4
+		x		x
8	-	2	x	7
+		-		+
6	÷	1	+	9

Solutions

21. TONGUE TWISTER
It is Ben.

22. BROOM, BROOM

24. SPOT THE DIFFERENCE

23. CHANGE A LETTER
1 Feel 2 Feet 3 Meet 4 Meat
5 Moat 6 Moan 7 Loan 8 Lean
9 Mean 10 Meal 11 Peal 12 Peel

25. NUMBER JIG

3	3	9	6	9		9	4	2	8	9	8
	0		4		5		1		1		
8	7	1		5	2	6		4	6	5	9
	8	2	3		1		8				5
		4				6	6	3	3	7	
	8	7	3	6	6	8			1		
4		5		5		3		1	0	7	
0		1		5	9	7	5	4		0	
2	4	3	7		0			6		0	
6		6			2	3	3	3	8	4	
2					4			7			
7	0	0	3		2	3	3	5	2	6	

26. CROSS OUT
```
L E M O N
I   A   I
L I N E N
A   G   T
C L O T H
```

27. CROSSWORDS

K	I	N	G	D	O	M		C	A	N	D	L	E
A		Y		I		A		P		L		O		V
R	U	L	E	S		G	R	A	T	I	T	U	D	E
D		O		C		I		D		A		B		N
A	N	N	O	U	N	C	E	D		S	U	L	K	
S				S				O				E		D
H	O	N	E	S	T		I	C	E	S	K	A	T	E
I		E		E		U		K		T		C		S
A	C	C	I	D	E	N	T		T	A	C	T	I	C
N		K				E				I				E
	P	L	O	P		A	F	T	E	R	N	O	O	N
B		A		I		R		R		C		B		D
O	R	C	H	E	S	T	R	A		A	R	E	N	A
O		E		C		H		M		S		S		N
K	I	S	S	E	D		P	R	E	S	E	N	T	

SPARKLE

28. HIDDEN WORDS

1 Many lo**CAL F**olk raise money for charity.

2 Mind you don't s**KID** on the ice.

3 Don't let the door s**LAM B**ehind you.

4 S**CUB**a diving is great fun.

5 A **CHIC K**aftan is very fashionable.

6 Chec**K IT TEN** times first.

29. PYRAMID PLAY

9, 1, 14, 4, 11, 6, 3, 13, 2, 8, 5, 12, 7, 10

30. JUNIOR SUDOKU

4	1	2	3	5	6
5	3	6	1	2	4
6	5	4	2	1	3
3	2	1	6	4	5
2	6	5	4	3	1
1	4	3	5	6	2

1	2	5	6	3	4
3	6	4	2	5	1
6	1	2	3	4	5
5	4	3	1	2	6
2	5	1	4	6	3
4	3	6	5	1	2

6	5	3	2	4	1
2	1	4	6	5	3
4	2	6	1	3	5
1	3	5	4	2	6
3	6	2	5	1	4
5	4	1	3	6	2

31. POND LIFE

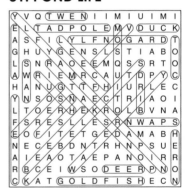

32. QUEST

1 Cubs **2** Boat **3** Zeta **4** Hour
5 Golf **6** Dali **7** Dots **8** Moth
9 STARFISH

Solutions

33. FUNNY BONES

34. KRISS KROSS

HORN

35. DOT TO DOT
It's a frog.

36. PICTURE PAIRS
4 and 5 are the same.

37. PICK ME UP
2, 5, 3, 8, 7, 6, 12, 10, 11, 9, 1, 4

38. MAGIC MIRROR
There are forty-two triangles.

39. ARROWORDS

		T	F	A	H		B
S	T	I	R	A	M	P	E	M	M	A
A		I	L	L	R	A	R	E	K
F	L	E	A	S	K	I	O	N	C	E
K		L	I	E	L	A	D	D	E	R
Z	O	O						N	
V		E					R	I	T	A
H	E	W	N			R		R	G
R	I	D				B	I	T	E
L					S	O	S
B	A	L	D				S	
L		A			C	O	S	T
P	A	S	T	A	A	U	R	U
S	W	A	N	M	A	N	S	I	O	N
O	G	Y	C	E	V	E
C	L	O	S	E	D	P	L	A	N	E
A	P	P	L	E	P	I	E	T	R	Y
K	A	S	P	P	A	R	A	D	E
K	E	E	N	P	I	E	R	L	O	T

40. OUT OF ORDER
11, 3, 18, 9, 5, 13, 1, 10, 15, 6, 12, 14, 8, 17, 2, 4, 16, 7

Solutions

41. SUGURU

3	2	4	2	4	3
4	1	3	1	5	1
2	5	2	4	3	2
1	3	1	5	1	5
2	5	4	3	4	2
4	3	1	2	1	3

41. SET SQUARE

2	+	1	x	5
+		+		-
6	-	9	+	7
+		x		+
4	x	8	+	3

42. CHANGE A LETTER
1 Vane 2 Vine 3 Mine 4 Mane
5 Mare 6 Mark 7 Park 8 Part
9 Past 10 Last 11 Vast 12 Vase

43. NATURE TRAILS
James is gathering hazelnuts.
Emma is picking blackberries.
Kevin is looking for mushrooms.

44. SPOT THE DIFFERENCE

45. CROSS OUT
S C O O P
P   N   R
O L I V E
R   O   S
T O N G S

Solutions

46. HAUNTED HOUSE

47. CROSSWORDS

CAMP WOLFGANG

48. CODEWORD

```
J E W E L   M   Q U I Z     B
A   A   E   E M U     O V A L
C L I M A T E   A L S O   S
K   S   S   T A R   A   P I G
P O T A T O   R   F A L S E
O   N   C I T Y   E   A   N
T A N G L E   A   O R A N G E
  G   E   A L L O W   B   E
G O B L I N   O   N O O D L E
A   A   D   K N E E   U   A
T A S T E   A     R O T T E R
E L K   A   R U N   X   E N
  T   F L E A   E C L I P S E
H E R E     T A X   I   E   S
  R   E D G E   T   P L E A T
```

49. QUEST

1 Hiss **2** Help **3** Pisa **4** Bear **5** Talk **6** Heel **7** Dice **8** Hour **9** SPARKLER

50. CAMPING

51. MAGIC BOXES

POLE	SPAN	ALPS
OVEN	POLE	LOOT
LEND	ALTO	POLE
ENDS	NEON	STEW

Solutions

52. PICK ME UP
7, 5, 1, 4, 10, 2, 9, 12, 3, 13, 6, 11, 8

53. KRISS KROSS

```
T O M   D E A D B E A T   T
U   I   E     E N   H O W
G R A S S L A N D   T   R E
B   S   I   U N E Q U A L
I   I   V   C   N   S   V
N   O V E R S T I T C H   E
E   N   R   I   E     B
  C A L Y P S O     D A D
D   R   E   N     F   L
I   Y A P P Y   E D I B L E
S   B       X   L   E
C L I M B T   H   L A R K
  A   E R R   A   Y   I
  Z A N Y   A   L     N
  Y       H Y S T E R I C A L
```

ACCIDENT

54. COUNT ON ME
There are eleven teddies.

55. DOT TO DOT
It's four fish.

56. NUMBER JIG

```
    3 6 3 4   2 4 3 8
    4   0         3
    9 5 0 4 9   8 3 8 8
6       6     4 0 2   8
1 2 1 1 3     1   3   1
4       5     7 1 4 8 7 2
6 7 5   1     1       2
0   7   7     8 6 1 8 4
4 4 5 4 7     1       3
  2   8   3 3 3 3 1 2
1 1 1 2 5 6   0       7
  7   0   3 2 7 5   5
```

57. CHANGE A LETTER
1 Cope **2** Cape **3** Café **4** Case
5 Cash **6** Cast **7** Cost **8** Post **9** Pose
10 Rose **11** Hose **12** Hope

58. JUNIOR SUDOKU

```
5 4 6 1 2 3
3 1 2 5 6 4
6 3 5 4 1 2
4 2 1 6 3 5
1 5 3 2 4 6
2 6 4 3 5 1
```

```
6 5 4 1 3 2
1 3 2 4 5 6
5 4 1 2 6 3
3 2 6 5 1 4
2 6 5 3 4 1
4 1 3 6 2 5
```

```
4 5 6 3 2 1
3 2 1 4 6 5
2 3 4 1 5 6
6 1 5 2 4 3
1 6 2 5 3 4
5 4 3 6 1 2
```

59. SUGURU

```
1 2 1 3 1 2
4 5 4 2 4 3
3 2 3 1 5 2
1 4 5 4 3 1
2 3 1 2 5 4
1 5 4 3 1 2
```

Solutions

59. SET SQUARE

4	+	8	x	9
x		x		÷
7	-	3	÷	1
+		+		-
5	x	2	-	6

60. PICTURE PAIRS
3 and 5 are the same.

61. EASTER EGG HUNT

62. SQUARE PAIR
B5 = A6, E8 = A9, E6 = G6,
E3 = C8, G1 = D4, A2 = C4

63. HOT STUFF

64. QUEST
1 Bike **2** Dawn **3** Hurt **4** Hour **5** Tuna
6 Open **7** Epic **8** Huge
9 ENTRANCE

Solutions

65. SPOT THE DIFFERENCE

69. SUGURU

5	2	1	3	4	3
1	3	5	2	1	2
4	2	1	4	3	4
1	5	3	2	1	5
3	2	4	5	3	2
1	5	1	2	4	1

66. PICK ME UP

11, 7, 5, 9, 1, 10, 2, 4, 6, 8, 3

67. CROSSWORDS

SINGLE WISH

69. SET SQUARE

6	x	7	-	9
+	■	+	■	+
5	-	1	x	3
+	■	-	■	-
4	-	2	x	8

68. OUT OF ORDER

2, 9, 14, 3, 11, 1, 10, 4, 7, 13, 6, 12, 5, 8

70. STRICTLY BALLROOM

Solutions

71. CROSS OUT

```
C R E A M
L   A   E
A N G E L
S   L   O
S T E R N
```

72. KRISS KROSS

```
B I K I N I   T H I C K E N
R     N     N   H       G
A     O     H O I S T   O
S U C H   E   R   I   S U
S   K   D R E S S M A K I N G
        I   T   E   A   P
T O A S T   A L   K   T   P
O       O   A L   E   P
F R Y   U N S A L E A B L E
N       C   M   P   O   T
F A N G   E M B L E M A T I C
D       L   R   I   Z
H O N E Y C O M B   A D M I T
O       N   E   E   N
T O Y   E N C O U R A G E
```

UNICORN

73. MAGIC MARIGOLD

```
B K W T C J E S E N A M Z X D
I N A I S H P Y F S T E B I T
Y I G D C L L R I P O L D T I
L A H A E N I U O E C L D R R
M V N N E E J R T L I G O B M
S A D V N K O E T L R A G T I
P O A D E W H Y A S U N I E C
R E U N I C O R N L O T R D S
H S L U F E C A R G O N A R A
T S P O I T E N A R S U M E O
I E E A T G M A B F E B S C D
Z N X V R L E G W A R M E R S
A I N T O K R H Y T U A E B S
P F U I S O L O T E P A C L N
F H O R N E H E I S O A T S Y
```

74. CHANGE A LETTER

1 Farm **2** Warm **3** Wart **4** Part
5 Past **6** Vast **7** Fast **8** Fact **9** Face
10 Fare **11** Fire **12** Firm

75. NUMBER JIG

```
      9   6 2 5 8
2 8 2   6       8
4   3   4 5 9 7 0   3
5 6 5 1 7   1     1 8 5
    1   1   1       7
9 3 2   2 6 8 8 0   7
      7   9     6 5 8
    5 7 3 2 5   8   2
5   2     5 7 2 7 0 0
2   1 3 0 5     0   2
1   3     6     5
7 0 5 3 0 2   7 8 8 8
```

76. SHED SOME LIGHT

77. CODEWORD

```
C R A W L   F   Q U I Z   J
A   P   O   E M U   O X E N
P E R F U M E   A M M O   W
I   O   S   T A R   A   F E W
T A N D E M   R E P T I L E
A   O   A R M Y   L   V
L A D D E R   A   D E L E T E
  I   G   R A D I O   Y   E
B R E E Z Y   A   U N R E A L
E   A   E   S M U G   I   A
A C R O B A T   H O C K E Y
D E N   R   A G O   A N   E
  L   K A R T   M I S H E A R
B L U E   U S E   I   E   E
O   Y U L E N   S A L A D
```

Solutions

78. JUNIOR SUDOKU

1	4	5	3	6	2
2	3	6	4	1	5
6	1	3	5	2	4
5	2	4	6	3	1
4	6	1	2	5	3
3	5	2	1	4	6

3	1	5	4	6	2
2	6	4	5	1	3
6	4	1	3	2	5
5	3	2	6	4	1
4	2	3	1	5	6
1	5	6	2	3	4

6	5	1	4	2	3
4	3	2	6	5	1
2	4	6	1	3	5
5	1	3	2	4	6
3	6	4	5	1	2
1	2	5	3	6	4

79. SINKING FEELING

80. QUEST

1 Pens **2** Talc **3** Zero **4** Yo-yo
5 Last **6** Five **7** Star **8** Owls
9 SCOOTERS

81. DOT TO DOT

It's an otter catching a fish.

82. PICTURE PAIRS

1 and 2 are the same.

83. CROSS OUT

```
M U S I   C
A     T   H
G L O V   E
I     R   S
C O M E T
```

84. SWEET SUCCESS

Solutions

85. SPOT THE DIFFERENCE

86. HIDDEN WORDS

1 To play this game you **GO BLIN**dfolded around the room.
2 Put the re**D RAG ON** the draining board.
3 In the sum**MER, MAID**s are employed at holiday camps.
4 It's the yellow t**UNIC OR N**othing.
5 Night pa**TROL L**eft the soldier feeling tired.
6 My neighbor has a teena**GE NIE**ce.

87. CROSSWORDS

V	A	N	I	S	H			U	N	W	R	A	P
A		O		W		S		B		E		A		A
C	A	B	L	E	T	E	L	E	V	I	S	I	O	N
A		L		L		S		G		N		T		T
T	R	E	A	T	M	E	N	T		H	A	S	T	E
I				N		C				T				D
O	H	A	R	E		T	R	A	P	D	O	O	R	
N		B		S		E		B		E		R		F
	O	U	T	S	I	D	E	R		C	O	M	M	A
I		N				U		O				O		M
C	A	D	E	T		S	U	P	E	R	H	E	R	O
I		A		H		I		T		A		M		U
C	O	N	G	R	A	T	U	L	A	T	I	O	N	S
L		C		E		E		Y		O		J		L
E	Y	E	L	E	T			B	R	A	I	N	Y	

HEAVENLY

88. SUGURU

1	3	2	4	1	4
2	4	1	3	5	2
1	3	5	2	1	3
2	4	1	3	4	5
3	5	2	5	2	1
2	1	3	1	3	4

88. SET SQUARE

4	x	6	÷	8
-		÷		-
1	+	3	x	5
+		+		+
2	x	7	+	9

Solutions

89. MAGIC BOXES

N O N E	K N I T	T H A N
O V E N	N O N E	H A L O
N E E D	I N K S	A L A N
E N D S	T E S T	N O N E

90. PICK ME UP

3, 6, 11, 1, 9, 2, 7, 10, 5, 8, 4, 12

91. KRISS KROSS

```
S T I C K I N G     B E A C H
P       O           E   R   O
L   C O M B   O B J E C T   S
A   O   E         E   T     P
S O M E T H I N G   L I P   I
T   M   O     I C E   A   T
I   O   U     N       T E   A
O       N           F L E A   L
C O N D I T I O N       E   C
U       E           T       I
S T O P   M I C R O C H I P
  C   U   U           I
  L   L   S     A C M E
R A M P   C L O T H   A
S       L       I     N
A S H A M E D   E M P E R O R
```

GOBLIN

92. SQUARE PAIRS

5C = 7F, 4E = 6B, 1B = 3B,
1E = 7D, 2F = 4A, 4B = 5G

93. CHANGE A LETTER

1 Cape **2** Cage **3** Case **4** Cast
5 Fast **6** Fist **7** List **8** Last **9** Past
10 Part **11** Cart **12** Care

94. NUMBER JIG

7	4	8	4	4		5		3	
6			2		6	5	3	4	0	1
3			3		6		1		6
1	2	4		2	8	3	5	2	6
3			8		1			3	7	2
3		7	0	0	7	6	7
8		8			6
1	3	1	7	1		5	7	7	5	0	5
6				5		6			0
6	6	7	9		4		9	7	3	7
3		2	2	6	3		6		6
4	1	7	2			5	1	7	2	4	6

95. QUEST

1 Wasp **2** Puma **3** Hiss **4** Alps
5 Damp **6** Zero **7** Four **8** Heat
9 PASSPORT

96. PICTURE PAIRS

2 and 3 are the same.

97. JUNIOR SUDOKU

4	1	6	5	3	2
5	3	2	6	4	1
6	4	3	2	1	5
2	5	1	4	6	3
3	6	5	1	2	4
1	2	4	3	5	6

4	6	1	5	3	2
5	2	3	4	6	1
2	1	5	6	4	3
6	3	4	2	1	5
3	5	6	1	2	4
1	4	2	3	5	6

1	4	5	6	3	2
3	6	2	4	5	1
6	3	4	1	2	5
2	5	1	3	6	4
5	1	6	2	4	3
4	2	3	5	1	6

98. CROSS OUT

```
F I R S T
L     A   A
A L I E N
M     S   G
E N E M Y
```

Solutions

99. SPARKLE

100. SPOT THE DIFFERENCE

101. NAME GAME

1 Office **2** Cereal **3** Equator
4 Snacks **5** Bakery **6** Person
FIREQUACKERS

102. SPLITZ

1 Banana **2** Erased **3** Orange
4 Acting **5** Smooth **6** School
GARLIC

103. MOUNTAIN MAZE

104. COUNT ON ME

There are twenty shoes.

105. CODEWORD

```
B L A S T   Z   M A Z E   V
A     L     I   E M U     G R I N
T O A S T E R     F L A G     X
H   R   L   O F F   W   J E T
T I M B E R     I   A L O N E
U   L   H O R N   K   I   L
B A K E R Y   A   K E N N E L
  G   E   M O T T O   A   A
T O P P L E   I   A B S O R B
E   L   E   T O O L   T     R
S Q U A D   H   A N Y O N E
T U G   G   I N K   I   C   A
  A   D E A R   N E G L E C T
A C H E     S K I   H   A   H
  K   N E W T   T   T E N S E
```

Solutions

106. STRICTLY BALLROOM

107. DOT TO DOT
It's a fish trying to catch a butterfly.

108. SQUARE PAIRS
C2 = F4, C4 = G7, D6 = G5, B6 = F2,
B4 = E6, D1 = F1

109. MAGIC BOXES

ECHO	PEST	WREN
CROP	ECHO	RICE
HOSE	SHOW	ECHO
OPEN	TOWN	NEON

110. FEELING FRUITY

111. HIDDEN WORDS
1 The firs**T RUN K**itty took part in
   was a success.
2 The fal**CON, E**agle, and hawk
   are birds of prey.
3 Bo**B RAN CH**arity events for local
   good causes.
4 Is a bobb**LE A F**ancy decoration
   on a hat?
5 My bes**T WIG** is a blonde one.
6 Good boots will la**ST UMP**teen
   years.

112. SPLITZ
1 Notice **2** Mayhem **3** Pepper
4 Sunset **5** Forget **6** Carpet
MAGPIE